From the Boundary Waters

From the Boundary Waters

Waters

Poems

Gordon Osing

Memphis State University Press

First printing credits for the following poems are with the following maga-
zines: "Auden" and "Ostinato" with the *Southern Review;* "My Grandma's
Back" with *Cimarron Review;* "Hoot Owl" with *racoon;* "At the School for
the Retarded" with *West Coast Poetry Review;* "Vachel Lindsay" with *Voices
International;* "Names, Love" and "Life Study" with *Raven;* "Adam's Ver-
sion" with *Louisville Review;* "The Catfish" with *Poetry Northwest;* "Topless
Dancer" with *WEVL Newsletter;* "The Veteran" with *Southern Voices;* "A Jap-
anese Garden in November" with *Xavier Review;* "To a Lady from the
Boundary Waters" with *Quilt;* "Song of the Scavenger" with *The Good Peo-
ple of Gomorrah* (St. Luke's Press, Memphis, 1979).

For M. J.

Thank you, Miller

I wish to thank the Walter R. Smith Distinguished Book Award Committee, specifically my colleagues Walter Smith, Kay Easson, and Lasley Dameron, for presenting the 1981 award to this work. Special thanks go to James Karsch for the pen and ink sketches.

Contents

III

And that this place may thoroughly be thought
  True Paradise, I have the serpent brought . . .

                              "Twickenham Garden"
                              John Donne

Your lost your innocence in one world, you can't
  regain it in another.

                              The Death of Artemio Cruz
                              Carlos Fuentes

Watch out for too much irony.

                              Letters to a Young Poet
                              Rainer Maria Rilke

Poetry may be merely an alteration of attitudes toward language, or it may be the extraordinarily conscious verbal ritual we all love, secretly or openly. I prefer Auden's naming it as that which "survives, a way of happening, a mouth."

Spiritual comedy, *sacer hilaritas,* is an essential ingredient of my voice, by which I mean a serious interest in the reader as well as in the lines of language, the images, the poem's disciplined shape, and the true taste of words.

That perfect moment that takes place in the mind, just before anything happens, can be turned completely into a language moment. Composition is pleasurable to me. I think the game is to make lines and phrases within a form conceived perhaps even before one received the kernel phrase or sentence of the poem. What it comes down to is that the style of the work is the theme of it, or at least the subject.

To the reader who prefers a more discussible notion of a theme let me offer: Innocence is the last ploy. Innocence is terror in disguise, denying involvement. Innocence is that empty beach glowing on a postcard. It is alienation seen through rose-colored glasses. And there is such a thing as a cry for guilt.

I hope I am speaking to a sizable audience of folks who are regrouping these days. In these horribly ersatz times. In these least political of most political times. In these heartless and sentimental times. In these compromised and scientized times. I hope the work strikes the reader as bread-and-butter poetry (with a little wine on the side).

The poems have been my escapes, simple and complex, but escapes from the clichés of seeing that are getting to be our sharable culture. For me they have been escapes into moments of most real living and meaning. Like the readers' own moments—larger, really, than the lives we are given to lead.

Envoi

I speak for those compelled around a throne
who grow a little weary of the song
and one by one steal back to be reborn.

I

Auden

The answer may be simple, but let's stay,
talk about it anyway, you might say,
a caduceus of smoke rising like a spirit
by your face, the fingers holding the cigarette
in incidental victory. More scraps than finished
words after all. And an avalanche of maps, diminished,
held in the wry traces of the mouth and in the skin
of the face itself, droll now as Original Sin.

Yours the Church of the Holy Rubble, Good Bishop Auden,
the childfully known, marvels, and the profaned forgotten.
Thou wert sillier than a bishop, and more proper
frowning from the playground to the sacristy door:
If the original idea was Sin, where does that leave
ideas about ideas? How love slaughters to forgive.

The Crows

What does the lord want, slick prayer
or injured words? For christ never melts
in my mouth. Nor does anything else.
I feel frozen to the ground, twisting air
for my going. And it is snowing now into the black
freshening waters at the center. The way back
is well known, yet the taking of these
waters makes one not so thirsty again
for any others.

       But that he sent the yellow wind
in the broken Fall sky where I recall his crows
aghast happily today in three pine trees,
in cross humor, lateral laughter/vertical clothes.
From time to time one circled to applaud
the way poems, broken prayers, go sideways to god.

My Grandma's Back

The first time I,
by the light of a kerosene lamp,
scratched my Grandma's back
with a corncob
from the bushel by the iron stove
in the living room
she said I couldn't do it hard enough
and loosened her coarse dress
so I could make bigger circles.

Thereafter I dreaded being asked
though as I aged
her quiet demand
and my ability to supply
equalized.

I never thought of this scratching
as anything but crude,
impossible to be told, even to one who knew her,
with her oval face, thick glasses,
gray hair grabbed into a bun
and the habit of chewing on her tongue.

For gratitude I had sighs and groans
her pleasure having happened
quite apart from my language.
I was glad I could never see her face.

I always looked with all my might
at the cast iron frills on the stove,
at the scheme in the linoleum,
at the wallpaper,
or as a very last resort
at the curious patterns of white lines
(or even tiny rows of red)
on her back.

Hoot Owl

As if you were an uncaused echo
you ask always the same
question of the evening,
your eyes always at the center
of your own night.

In the beginning when I stand
in the middle of the sand road past
the home place
you call in the distant woods
and the evening turns still darker blue,
the fields growing thicker
around your cry.

In this town, too, tonight you muse
and, city or no city, the mind
circles out into groves.

You are out there somewhere
on the rim of my ears.
Someone inside me opens the eyes still wider and begins
looking for movement in the gone day.

At the School for the Retarded

Like immigrant dolls
whose eyes are behind scrubbed faces
these five young girls are round old peasant dames
bantering and scolding through the waiting room
in shawls and black coats yet in April.

They have their last age first.
They cross the room turning and nodding to one-another
as if they belonged to an order.
Four keep fists deep in their pockets;
one holds hands with herself.

They've made the beds and scrubbed the floors in "D"
and go where they are already
reckoned by patient smiles.

"Soon," he says, "they may handle change in the drug
   store.
Later they will take walks in town alone.
Eventually, of course, they will be still
children."

The Fox

Lost deeper than his lair,
what does the fox in the well
think about
when the boys return
holding rocks?

Everything is prayer.

Pick-Up-Sticks

(for Mike Feehan)

Say Faith takes up hovering snakes—
well nose in here with your eyes—kneel
where the fist releases so many needles—
rouge ones, lemons, green ones, blanks—
to fall in webs stacked like remembering—
weightless—wooden theories of lace—mind's hand frees
careful as a camera—can't hold back too much
and still pick—know when to take back the touch.

It's neither webs nor lace, but erected hills, stick sprees.
Withal a fanged inertia in the blamed things
lift at the points touching; clear the pile until
the can's filled. Forget the eyeless gods of sheer weight
sleep all the time. You bite smiles and beat
them, damn, they sleep more deeply still.

Afraid

My friends think I'm angry as sulphuric acid,
what they drink in hell. But this is ridiculous.
I'm afraid of the undersides of these armored magnolias.
I'm afraid standing so close to a freight train
my body feels wheels.
I'm afraid of the pure solutions singing in the tips of
    flames.

I'm afraid as fire is of snow
and of the vast, frozen, brilliant night.

I fear the old maps of Paris that reside in decaying leaves.
I'm always afraid as roots scattering underground,
as the mad sprinkles of rain all up and down Blythe Street,
where I live.

What world will exist when I am no longer afraid
is the same one that already gleams around us
a slaughtered Buddha in every nook and cranny
all turning clear as *aqua vitae*.

So is an old story continually cleansed away
as with a water that burns.

Vachel Lindsay

Prophet out of Paradise,
nothing in the house on Fifth Street
explains your eyes
or your ideals
or the thirty-three years
of your humiliation.
You revelled in the glory
of William Booth,
sang more than you listened
to tell the truth.

They made you their flag
to wave and show and put away.
You strode and pranced,
called them to greatness, chanting,
disbelieving the darkness that must come,
the throat tangled with the lye
they gave you to drink.
. . .

As every moondrawn stem is true to its least known
    purpose
on a Winter afternoon in Washington Park
as for the first time, I knew you.

Sunburned foliage waved wildly like hands in heaven.
The ducks hovered in low ground by the road.
Your pavilion was Chinese and dark as closed eyes.

We could not bait the black swan to the rocks
with popcorn or the pleas of children.
The pond was his only as, apart, he glided
content his presence was enough
without the gabble and the grab
for bits of food along the edge.
From time to time the head and arched neck
dipped sinuously down
to taste of the cold, brown water.
To his true, gleaming day
the carillon hung tunes
so delicately mad
in a raw, grey sky.

Hubcap Mandala

(for Diane Wakoski and Robert Turney)

Now that you have willed the body to be full
of the things around you
and only the hubcap still defies beauty
blinded by its having been a thing
more perfect than the simplest machines
and nearly thrown away by time
let us remember how you had to pry hard—
it was the last tight fit.

Remember jacking up the mass
flattening the wheel,
clanking in the nuts one at a time,
finally fixing it with the heel
one last lick.

Hung on nails now
to be knocked down reaching for the rake
and roll on the ground in a round line
coming centered singing down into itself.

Pick it up, see your face fished
and the rim fingers on the backside.

Let's see them all still hanging on
the garage, their signs still mythic:
Nash—that whirling word.
A pilgrim phantom shining in a shining sea.
The last one a pony, a wild thing
running in the silverest time.
Let's save them all as sacred loot.
Let's use the hubcap one more time
in our minds,
friends of mine,
and celebrate one-another to boot.

Jessica

is four by the great fireplace in the parlor
where a new fire climbs and whispers
through a little world of sticks
and the sun dances out of its thick cellar.
The log whitens, glows and burns, streams
sad light. She jumps as this world crackles,
laughs a little, folds her little fingers
and says in silly brilliance, Now, Fire, you are green!

Where she gazes in willed rapture, Heaven knows.
Her voice is a voice for a sister, her eyes freeze
and a cherub sinning is in her clothes.
She stamps her foot to fix in fire her pose.
It's a wise Daddy says, She doesn't always say please;
I always try to please her when she does.

Names, Love,

there's a world of things
that still don't have names.

The motion of a maestro's hand
exciting the strings,

the time between I pinch my finger in the pliers
and the pain,

where thighs end
the tender little valleys
of silken skin.

Oh there are still things, Sweet,
that have no names.

Picture of a Lady

It breaks the heart with pleasure and with loss
the way you come down from the October hill
riding the old logging road on your golden "Dude."

Your light hair is set to the sides of your face
and held in the back; you're wearing your green
wool jacket.

(Years later, you're smiling just now
thinking of me writing this tonight.)

You sit easily on his sleek shoulders.
You are flushed, but the soft line of your mouth
is an unbroken horizon in a land of slow streams.

Your eyes look inward, down
where he steps
alive in his bright, slick legs

toward where I wait (even as I pause now)
the light coming in lines
under the trees beneath a changing sky.

And I see you are complete within yourself,
forever at the exquisite distance if you never arrive.

Adam's Version

(for Etheridge Knight)

In the beginning I had to invent
myself, and it was darker, deeper
in those days. On the darkest of them
I couldn't come out of my cave
though all the world were Eve
wanting love. Well I wept a good deal.
Nights were a complete victory of the horrors.
As it turned out, actually,
only the insane thrill of dying, over and over,
kept me going. Until I remembered
more and more, little by little,
and I actually began to learn the others.
I came to enjoy fresh fruit.
I learned to think with my nose in the boudoir,
with my ears among friends,
and with my ass, like the rattler, other places.
The stranger I get, in other words,
the saner they think I am.
Well I do get tired of the dog wearing all my faces.

The Catfish

(for Parker Rushing)

Dusk, the trees and brush around the shore,
the dank air over the pond, hoot-owls,
and unseen jitterings through the shadows
were all around us, cluttered, like a language.
We rowed along the trotline saying nothing.
I reached ahead of the bow to be the first
to the mystery tugging our sunken line.

And see me there, after we'd lifted the thing
fluttering into the boat, noting with the others
the wit of the hook, the torn mouth,
and kneeling in the bottom of the boat,
holding with both hands, even leaning on
this two pound cat. It was Europe clutching Asia
in an old *Times* cartoon.

You talked me out of fearing his dull croaking,
the twitching head and distended fins.
I made him fit my hand, put his head down
into our old blue speckled coffee pot.
While we rowed toward the car he thrashed and died
ingloriously vertical. By candlelight I slit him
into the spring,

and held him up for study, turning him slowly.
He was slipping along the bottom, his whiskers alive,
his eye as murky as his movements curved.
And he was all sleek, his belly a white sheen,
his head amazed.

II

Tremors

(for Jackson Baker)

Something just becoming sound
fills the bottom of everything.
The lake of fear is suddenly drained.
The evening is loaded with the darkness of a tunnel.

Earth's silence is coming loose
and the place is about to dance
the dead on strings.

If not this time.

(Still, on the third evening
a dark chanting rises in my feet and legs

and the day inside me slips
sand over gravel inside my thighs

and begins to be
bruised like the inside of thunder

and moves
the very bottom of music.)

Digressions

(for Parker Rushing)

In an adjoining room
there are any number of doors,
a detective's heaven,
into adjoining rooms,

thus a forest of doors
no saw ever buzzed.

You hold it is slippage,
I say things err splendidly forever.
It comes out a crawdaddy
always going northeast or southwest,

or like light bending,

or like a right-handed river
learning to use its left.

Topless Dancer

(after a photo by Diane Arbus)

I make, plus tips, one big bill every night
and, as Daddy always said, nothing on earth
is worth more than a hundred dollars,
not even the sad little electric sun
I always have with me for my feet.
I put on my gowns careful of the frayed cord
and the unforgiving touch of the orange heat.

Oh the picture there by the mirror, maybe;
I tore out the middle part years ago,
or the sides dropped off from putting it away
every time. You can't see the hands
is all you miss. But the face is the best part
anyway, you might say. It's The Last Supper,
Leonardo baby. You like my gold sheath?

It shows my boobs great. Guys have told me
I look like several stars. My face don't change
when the lights turn on me. This is how I work.
Near the end of my act I start twirling my tits
and the eyes out there are doing the old razzamatazz.
I really shine their eyes for them, scramble their eggs.

Boys, I say when the best part comes,
you sonsabitches, come and get it.
But they just stare glued to their chairs.
I mean this is a nice place to work,
none ever do.

Matinee

(for Tom Carlson)

Back in the old days when you could come in twice,
in the middle, in that beginning, in that one instant
that must happen twice, that you've seen before
but hadn't known a future as its cause,

in that split second before knowing
in the one-way dark, delight showing on a far white
wall (the marquee blinks blindly through the day,
billboards peel back stories to the bricks),

in the one moment that cannot, by odds, happen,
has, someone raises an unknowing left hand
into another story continually disappearing,
only the past happening, albeit Zeus-like wisdom

crashes happily in the plate glass flat
afternoon in the avenue, slick lobby stills
telling it all, every outcome a beginning,
that seam the fingers find following form,

that you dread/love, the cold ring shining
the moment theatre turns theatre again,
others coming in. Remember that thunderous daylight
in the eyes, the nameless heat that seized the skin.

At One

It's late, it's early, so with those choosing old movies,
where they've studied something like each other, which
   proves
we see them double, let me share a post-ultimate thought
not so sentimental and cruel as old Procrustes' cot.
(We're guilty enough of Heavens, lowest bidders, too,
til some have needed to plead *Nicht schuldig, nicht schuldig*.)
It's one o'clock now in the actual A.M..
Ayatollahs of the airways and late-late dramas
infest the dark screen. All the town's beautiful temples
are empty, and I'm finishing this last wrinkle
so it is the twenty-fifth hour. What's done
is, perforce, shared perfectly with someone. Red-handed
I am left to choose the not-necessarily planned.
The small hours and a thick daybreak are just begun.

The Sheep

There are those who have never heard
of a mad sheep,
for they are all mad
where they graze
in ruined energy
crowned by the bright sky.

Each is a peace
of himself.
They are all, each and all,
old River Kings

who waged war their whole lives long
in order to flash the greatness of the peace
they desired

who made laws
thicker than the hoary forests
they wore on their backs,
on their wine-plump skins

whose souls now fill the blue skies,
become one shadow at night
till it is time again
to kiss the daylight
whole worlds in their eyes.

They seem earth-clouds
dwelling over the hills and valleys.

The awful mind of each
is a gorgeous beast.

Legends

Up where I'm from they remember
ones too much their kind
kept in the attic.
The Law would have to come,
just one of the law's mistakes.

In Ireland all the air is full of snakes.

The Veteran

It's true some guys come back worse off than me
but it doesn't help. With no fingers I'm a freak.
Everything's blasted round, anything is a trick.
My wrists are tied. A moon-face burns horribly.

Gone tasting the shapes of things. To be blunt
people can have what they reach for is a crock.
The world I see is all a busted clock.
I lift a club to everything I want.

I have to muscle a cup of coffee. My days are maimed.
But night is the worst. I churn; sometimes I dream
I'm feeding tigers. I start, and my arms are obscene.
My woman turns to me and I'm ashamed.

The Crux

(for Miller Williams)

Whatever it was Orpheus feared in his own songs
that he sang his way unwaveringly down
into the other world,
he could not call his love into the light.

Grown hungry on the tightening distance between them,
on sheer promise,
on her need
that he should love her more than the command

until she stopped, he felt himself turning,
changing before her,
losing his memory.
He knew singing to be seeing things dying

into their larger lives, fearing the loss of her
he dare not see
even as he saw her
descending, back into the momentary gleam.

on the living skin of the sinuous one
that moves by never moving in itself
in a place where the ground itself is suddenly wise,
that turns into a world that bears his face.

The Python

Glassed in
what is, if not chagrin,

despair
he blunts the fetid air

the zoo
contains and scarcely moves.

He'd seem
a root, our sourest dream

with eyes
that one hates in surprise.

How few
the things he lives to do.

How wise,
elaborate his guise.

The Diamond

If, after all the hatred and the precision,
the stars are still
the stars, and every word contains a curse

or a blessing, down where it lies
like another world
in the heart, darkness drifts

out from under the cooling leaves
not unlike the way
evil wisdom uncoils itself slowly in the yellow sun.

Not unlike walking backwards into oneself
the love grows still
smaller, harder every day.

Not unlike something crushed smooth and clear
what is out there is perfect in each of its parts

if, like the night skies, it speaks
only in the languages of the eye.

Coming Off the Highway
at the End of Summer

Three hundred plus across the bottom of the hot
afternoon, and the eyes remain behind
in the grey, rough symmetry of every angle
to the wizened barn, its cool darkness
giving in every way to the circling line
of the sun; in the dry beds that remain
in the corners of the eye, in the cold plumes
of cloud, last catching the light, foretelling
that pure night in the Fall

the mist comes ahead of the chill in the orchards,
the stars apple-sweet, the moon a blade
caring less even for serpents
than for its own perfection, glowing carefully
over the silence steaming breath.

Before the barbed fences lie in low curls
half-buried by the rubble of the graders,
and the weather is the song of it all,
the breathing seasons,
when, like episodes recurring in an unlived life,
the back country goes on, thickening
and bearing white.

With the forgotten begin all the things that are true
if this evening even the body would go to seed,
homing anywhere. Earth lover.

The old guy said today at the station,
This year the groves are going to take
all the rain and snow they need;
the days of the blind snake are nearly over.

III

To a Lady from the Boundary Waters

Coming out from where we landed on the edge
of Duluth, M. J., the first thing I saw was the mist
filling the birch and pine woods,
and I remembered bathing my face in your hair.

Yesterday walking alone a long time
in the dense cool of forest sunlight
(called perfectly in the cold trill of the loon)
I remembered being in your eyes, brown and yellow
and green.

I love your North.
Even now as I am writing
the birches are giving their white papers to the sun
so slowly you never see it happen,

the surface of the water is weaving
a design no one will ever put on,

all the thousands of little tongues of the forest
are laughing and you can barely hear a thing.

Killer Harmonies

(for Jerry Lee Lewis)

In Hell they hang a man on the evidence of a dried apple.
He jumps down and they're off searching again,
all this, of course, without any ending end.
Luther thought of it. It makes life sacramental
bliss and terror. Gives the old soul a little juice.
And so do you; so give those keys hell, Jerry Lee.
Sing's what we do best. Smoke-filled lights tease
and hold hard love among all forbidden fruits.
More Hindu than a jukebox in your glittering hands
you know about the bloody gears of the mind.
You know there'll be assholes in Heaven, many blind
heroes—and you, the Johnny-Apple of all Seedy Pianos.
There old songs hang in the air, Killer, over dazzling
    pleasures
here at ground zero, long since spoiled by gods, clean to
    the last measure.

Luther

*Therefore it is God's justice which justifies us
and saves us. And these words became a sweeter
message for me. This knowledge the Holy Spirit
gave me on the privy in the tower.*

Martin Luther

"Best it always all goes away. Never mind,
the seasons were in your eyes all the time.
Better the days roll like heads, the hours
like peaches in a tub or the lurid purity flowers
have for a little. What stays are the nameless
and innumerable days, patterns blameless
as the weather, rusted as sacred in their sly sameness.
It's good to leave Heaven for the earth it always proves.
What breaks so well into millions of pieces as love's
heart for reasons. Let go having it ever the same.
Hear the hint of sacred laughter in every single name.
The secret music surrounds you, wind in chimes."

"Inkwells and farts to you, *Bescheissen,* as Jahweh holds
    words
on Saturday afternoon in the privy sacred; wills them
    swords."

Bescheissen is Luther's familiar name for Satan. The word conjures
    "divine excrement."

Two Falconers: A Chinese Wall Hanging

(for Robert Bly)

In the bright silk moving
two small free birds play in the distance,
one resting perfectly in the top
branch, the other crucified ecstatically
upside down, diving ecstatically
in the ancient yellow air.

Two falconers stand life-size
in dark lines before us. On the left
the goshawk is at the ready, his wings lifted,
waiting in his master's smile

while the other lord is astonished to find time
has brought back a warless bird the first painter
delighted to put there where a sharp-eyed dove
shades perfectly the hawk with folded wings
at the right hand. He raises the left to speak

and the first knight carefully listens.
Through the forked tree in the background between them
and through the faces and the raiment of both men
a mountainside rains gently in the distance.

Franz Klammer

(for Roger Easson)

He comes carrying in his hands
the spear of an enemy.
He leaps up like a man
into the cold discovery, and humbles himself
descending into the fixed grace and risks
of the long, terrible, meandering dance
to the last line.
How the path climbs inside the mind
and the antiphonal flurry of faces.

He turns swiftly from time to time
as to the loveliest one in an old dance
and gives blind ears to everything
save the victory in his temples
and the obedient mysteries of his body.
He pulls a whole world down behind him
in his wild escape.

He proceeds in his race
like the splendid thoughts of a blind man
reciting the past.
The thoughtless watch
is the name of the game
and there are more ways than one
to whip the best time.

He is determined to win
walking seventy miles an hour.
He is all over the mountian
on instant legs.

He raises up one leg
childishly lost over its own fast floor,
then taught immediacy.
He flies out briefly airborne
and lands turning, stepping sideways,
oppressing the white
into blind scrolls, a mist
up from the wit of his knees.
He sews up the day
with the helter-skelter melodies in his knees.

He flies down through the shimmering day,
down over his frozen desert river path.
The many wishful minds
tighten his skin. The wind
loves totally his face and hands,
as the white mountain does the empty sky.
He lives in his serene riding
furiously down over his own rough rails.

He has memorized service to the old time
and he finishes his run still pumping,
easing up sideways beyond the finish,
in the circle of the others,
knowing among them,
full of the world's breath,
readying himself
for the next time.

Mandala for Planting a Flower Bed

(for Kay Easson)

Where last year a bee disappeared precisely
into eye after eye of a whole line of blue flowers

the shining and the silence in the seed
go before, again, the impassioned season

and here brilliant rags of color
will sing in the mind's eye like certain moments

as if to say the brain need fear nothing more
than the violence of a stain

nor love anything less
than the tangles yet in the trees

that build the shade of the flowers glowing
more richly than the master light of days

a living lace all around
their opening and closing like pleasured eyes

soundless and kindling the measured hours of earth
out of timeless ground.

Song of the Last Pretty Girl

(for Linda Bridges)

As surely as a preacher loves a widow, beyond
honesty there is something else, if betrayed
totally as ten blind babies for fingers
on a padre's arm. The lavender ladies
give it all there in the steps, slightly
more than there is. Well the moon is just a thing
at *our* right ears. If a bar of soap makes us
the same I'm the one who comes clean.

As a matter of fact, surely as evil is part praise, too,
we unlucky saints labor in the harder glory
of painted, silent lights, and rich stories.
The things still beyond the things that are true
keep furnishing blind homilies to the tongue,
and fancy disrelations, big-eyed song.

Song of the Scavenger

If under the iron green lids I discover
each time what has always been known,
the beggar is, nevertheless, beneath me,
turning in his dull fingers an old hat of someone's

in merely his latest need; like the frail rich
able to love only the solitude in things.
The beggar, who calls even the dogs Sir!
stepping menacingly from the shade of buildings.

In my hands, finally, things have become
what they are. My work is like History itself.
Indeed, I feel like talking a language beyond language.
(For I reject the graceless innocence of the beggar.)

I feel like talking your language. The hot smells
and the rains are not so senseless as his hand
who gives all away for his one silent question,
who, at best, in his art of asking almost stands.

Everything comes easily at last into my song.
Imagine I may be surprised at any time,
my glance made solely of innocent complicity
and grace of smallest things, intricate, a cat's tongue.

The Ducks

Back and forth at the edge
of the brown water in the park
the black chow barks

where the ducks
have hurried with lifted wings
and set sail for the center

as if to say: Sir, have your speed
(so that we make it to the water).

What is it to us whether you know
we are secretly terribly busy
gliding before your greed.

The Wyndham Sisters—Sargent

(for Cyd)

How to make these three ladies think of me—
I'm in the glass like a thought; as certainly
they are in your mind there—I see you thinking them
inside the whorehouse rouge and filigree of the frame,
a jungle of a parlor behind their gowns,
all satin, the faintest rose or white. Bright tunes
are in their curls, hidden ribbons. A hinted grin
of private knowing in each—one cognac, one whiskey, one
    wine—
matches the display of hands. Whose unseen looks
    backward,
bird-like, happily sad. Apart subtly, the eldest orders
laughter. The youngest's smile nourishes, like the mother's,
seeming stained glass or Spanish, framed above her,
mostly a blue-gowned ghost filling the half-dark.
The Wyndham Sisters wait timelessly one's next remark.

A Japanese Garden in November

In honor of the secrets that are around us openly,
friends, we stand together here on a frozen path
like the releasing circle of numbers in a combination.

Cold sunlight washes the eyes clear.
Yellowing leaves search in circles
over the ground everywhere.

Bless the bright edges that fill the sky,
bless the rake of the wind.

Bless the strength of those who love in fear.

Bless the playful mind.
Curse the humility of those who turn away,
curse the callous kind.

Bless the arc of the red bridge
always the same.
Bless the actual life.
Bless the blooms
that sit upon the undulating green
leaves upon a cool darkness
trailing roots down into a shining immense.

Our faces do what we see; our eyes are sweet.
How fine our speaking in this gold and winding place.

". . . you may already have won . . ."

Do not forgive, nor ask to be forgiven
and one is suddenly in the center of what is neither
a first class hell, especially, nor a junk heaven,
says the birds' singing, each in some correct dress
of this place, being of such-and-such kinds
already in their one-time wilderness.

Even as they touch the mind's ear too much
salvaged in the branches, and in the rich duties
of an old house. So I, too, carry out ashes,
stain and stir to lush ditties on the radio.
I load the dishes, garden and seat chairs,
make the bed (the sheets billow coming even,
sing softly in the fingers). Weathers demur;
brick antique walls guard my sweeping the back stairs.

Life Study

Strength is an earthly monster, I make no preten-
sions to it. My force, whatever there may be of it,
is altogether spiritual.

The Artist of the Beautiful
Nathaniel Hawthorne

How kind were the attentions of my friends
that first year of my salvation,
though they could see from day to day
my right eye descending in my face
and becoming an ellipse, blue-silver like sky,
while the left eye migrated
to above where the right one had been
and became an eye-within-triangle,
the very sign of triune omniscience.

Eventually they joined the others in awe;
I avoided mirrors.

Then the quake inside my face
and the right side of my mouth
no longer lined up with the left.
My nose became a seven on its side.
It was just as well. By the end of the second year
I couldn't even talk about the weather anymore.

By the end of the third
my face had become perfectly round,
a final adjustment I'm sure, and glowed pink-orange.
My hair and beard had bloomed into a sunburst,
my ears become a bow-tie by my chin.

At that point they all chipped in and got me
a little mountain pretty far from town.
I didn't have the heart to tell them
my torso and arms and legs and fingers and toes
had turned all to cylinders and sinew
under my clothes.

It's not that I'm hindered, mind you. In a sense
I'm more together now than ever. And I wish
they'd come closer when they drive out
to find me on the morning sky with their binoculars.
They think I'm waving a blessing for their flesh.

So, alas, I don't feel exactly transported
like some Turk. It turns out Salvation
isn't salvation either,
but just more work.

Song of the Thief

Everything is mine, for I own nothing
except the backs of everyone's eyes,
who see nothing until it is gone
in a split-second empty as a window shines.

At the moment of the bright fingers
something disappears into all your minds
and you know it. You look everywhere
else. You love the fiction in anything,

the invisible in things. But too late!
My law of one demands, all time supplies.
My gift is that empty place in the corner;
my coin gleams in the corners of your eyes.

For what can belong to any if I own it all
being simply unbelievably honest. You see
with new eyes each time. An interior counting
is suddenly altered. The only thing missing is me.

Leftovers

(for Phil Castille)

Meals on time we were calling the bourgeois god,
which called to mind the feasts of old religions,
which is what leftovers resemble. Someone part pope
can turn them into food of the next world
until you imagine very earth Heaven's refrigerator,
the shelves all but celestial with the remembered
onion, the pepper soup, numerous utterly altereds,
slightly like Jesus, raised or not by the third day.
Heaven, too, it turns out, is always the other place,
Japanese as the old flower smell in a theatre,
beyond the frigid air. Maybe it'll turn out
Hell is the overdone, and icebox stereos, oldies
in self defense. What did it mean to fear the loss
of things as they are? The hour to eat is sacred as the
    sauce.

Ostinato

The bones! The bones!
Robert Frost

No question the soul lives right in the bones
as every comic knows, and as nobody knows
the soul's name haunting the glass case in the lab
sans more than everything and deader than a desert.
The more thanks thereunto the lust that teacheth:
(Oh tend the great spangled tree of the night,
my bones!) It's the bones move in a song,
as in her sweet moral racket walking to the bath.
The way she walks tells all about the bones
in a tune, even as all her smiles are in the keys,
plus the dumb blood tune of the baseman's thumb.

A nasty holiness this life, these masks with skin.
We know and choose knowing as the wild ones do,
as in the magic counting seizing the drummer in his hands.